Cover Photo: Michael Symonds and Christopher Symonds in ***The Fine Print***, on stage at *The Promenade Theatre*, Los Angeles, June 2009.

Guilty Moments
© Arthur M. Jolly
Trade Edition, 2013
ISBN 978-1-934962-29-9

Also Available From
Original Works Publishing

FIVE FEARS OF FATHERHOOD

A short play collection by Michael Weems

SNIP - Did your last vacation include lying to your wife about an unsafely performed medical procedure? Did it involve your high level of intoxication and sheer disregard for body, family, health, and future? Did it really, really hurt for a week afterwards? No? Ted's did. Ted's got some explaining to do. (1M, 1F)

GOOD TALK - Every father dreads the day of 'the big talk' with his son. What happens when the son has a few secrets to reveal to dear old dad? (2M)

WHERE THE TRUTH LIES - An urban legend has come true. There once was a tale of a mysterious man, an enigma who turned men's lives upside down. They would lose sleep, gain weight, and find hair mysteriously gone white. He is... 'The Baby Maker' – natural ally to the ticking clocks of women and nemesis to modern man. Today, he's been spotted. Hide your wives... (4M, 1F)

FUZZY RED HAT - While most families are putting up the last stocking on Christmas Eve – Joe's night finds him in a rundown mall – attempting to convince Santa to reconsider his daughter's selfless Christmas wish. What do you do when 'Santa' is the one needing an infusion of holiday spirit(s)? (2M, 1F)

BOOK OF LOVE - Tara is a love machine. Tara is a love machine with a penchant for taking detailed notes immediately after her encounters. Tara is a love machine who is going to have that baby whether her hubby, Will, wants it or not. Tara is a love machine that's gone a little haywire and with only one route back to reality - Will. (1M, 1F)

Guilty Moments

An Evening of Short Plays

by

Arthur M. Jolly

Table of Contents

For my father.

Howie's Last Words

Cast: (1M, 1F)

HOWARD: A stuntman returning from a close call.
LACY: His concerned wife.

SETTING:
Written for a bedroom, but not specific.

TIME:
The play takes place in the present.

HOWIE'S LAST WORDS received its premiere Equity performance at the Annual Summer Shorts Festival, City Theatre, Miami, FL.
June 2nd, 2005.
The play was directed by Barbara Lowery
Cast was as follows:
Howard: Greg Weiner
Lacy: Shana Youngblood

AT RISE:

(A bedroom. LACY is sitting on the bed.)

(HOWARD enters.)

LACY: How'd it go?

HOWARD: Yeah.

LACY: What?

HOWARD: It was fine. I need a few minutes.

LACY: You stink.

HOWARD: It's the gel. I cleaned off as much as I could in the trailer, but I need a shower.

LACY: Yeah, you do. Smoke and chemicals.

HOWARD: I know. I just need my ten minutes, okay?

LACY: I missed you.

HOWARD: Jeez, Lacy, I was gone ten hours. Most people work every day.

LACY: I was worried.

HOWARD: Ten minutes, Lacy. I've got to have my ten, especially...

LACY: What?

HOWARD: Nothing. I'm getting in the shower.

LACY: So it went okay.

HOWARD: You asked that.

LACY: You don't look okay.

HOWARD: I'm here.

LACY: I was worried.

HOWARD: I know what I'm doing out there.

LACY: I know. I was just worried.

HOWARD: Yeah. It wasn't good.

LACY: Do I want to know?

HOWARD: Everything was fine, I just thought it was… The valve on the airtank screwed up.

LACY: While you were on fire?

HOWARD: Yeah. Or right before they lit me... whatever. They got the shot, I just got a little freaked.

LACY: Tell me.

HOWARD: Really?

LACY: I want to know.

HOWARD: We were on that soundstage in Brooklyn, it's the only one that lets you have open flames inside. I've got the little airtank on, 'cause it's gonna be a couple of minutes, tops, from hoods on to fire out and the hoods off. But the valve jammed, so instead of breathing from the tank, I'm breathing the air in this little pocket - trapped between the nomex and me. But as I'm sucking air in, it's pulling the fumes in from the fuel. That hexane glue, so while I was on fire, I was essentially sniffing glue. I started hallucinating, and I didn't know why, and I couldn't figure it out because I'm friggin' high on glue fumes.

LACY: Oh my God.

HOWARD: I just knew something was wrong, and I couldn't tell why or what, so I thought I must be dying. Burning to death. I remember going down, and Babs and Steve coming in with the extinguishers, and putting me out. I remember, very clearly, grabbing the hoods and ripping them off so I could breathe. I just had to get air, and I couldn't see. There were flashes of white, but I was blind. I didn't pull the hoods off.

LACY: I thought –

HOWARD: Yeah, I thought so too. Apparently, I was just lying there. Babs grabbed them - she pulled them off. She said my eyes were open, but she could tell I wasn't seeing anything. She thought I was blind. I remember pulling them off, though. I remember doing that. The worst thing was... after I could breathe, and I'm lying there, thinking they've put me out, and it's over and whatever went wrong, it's over, I'm okay... and then I heard it again.

LACY: What?

HOWARD: Flames. Fire from the inside. There's nothing else that sounds like that. It's like scuba diving, everything sounds different underwater? Everything sounds different inside fire, too. Only in the opposite way. ... So I heard the flames, and I realized I was still on fire, and they hadn't put me out at all, I had just hallucinated that they put me out, because I was so desperate for them to do it. And if I had hallucinated that, I was dying, because why else would I be hallucinating? So I threw myself down, and they put me out, and Steve or Babs grabbed the hoods and pulled them off so I could breathe, breathe that cold air, and I could taste the dust on the floor as I gulped great lungfuls of it. I'm lying face down, my cheek against the floor, I could taste the dust and I knew that I was going to be okay, and I knew that it was over and they'd put me out, and I was okay. And then... then I heard the flames again, and I knew I was still on fire and they hadn't put me out, I had hallucinated it and that meant that I was dying or dead, because if I was still on fire after all this time, I was dead. I wasn't hallucinating because I was burning, I was dead and reliving my death, and I threw myself down and they put me out and pulled the hoods and I breathed and I heard the flames and I was still on fire.

LACY : Jesus, Howie.

HOWARD: Five times. Five times, I swear to you, I would swear to God that they put me out and I knew it was over, and then I was back in it. After the fifth time, it stopped. I'd been getting enough oxygen. Maybe it was ten seconds later. Babs said, I fell forwards, they got me out and the hoods off in a few seconds, and I was on Oh-two seconds after that, and then I sat up and started asking what the hell happened.

LACY: You could've died.

HOWARD: I don't think so. Look at it rationally, we did the stunt, had a malfunction in the airtank - which is a major deal, I'll grant you - but everything worked out. The safety guys got me out, the medics were there if I needed them, but I didn't. A couple of minutes later, my head cleared from the fumes, and I realized everything was cool. One thing had gone wrong, but the safety backups did their job. We even got the shot. The only place this was serious was in my head, and that's because I was tripping, I couldn't think straight. It was a good stunt. I just got a bit freaked. Babs got me good on the way back.

LACY: What she do?

HOWARD: We were driving back to the workshop to drop off the gear, I was explaining what had gone on in my head, and she looked at me, in that cool, dykey way of hers and says "Howie, you do know you're still on fire, don't you?"

LACY: That's not funny.

HOWARD: You're telling me, I almost ran off the road. Just for a moment there...

LACY: Are you gonna quit?

HOWARD: What?

LACY: Are you gonna quit this?

HOWARD: The film?

LACY: Everything. Stunts.

HOWARD: And do what? It took me ten years to get where I am. I beat out fifty guys for this movie. People call me, Lacey, they call me. Chris Meyer's producing this one, it's like the fifth film I've done with him. He asked for me. I spent years getting to this point. I'm not quitting now.

LACY: What about next time?

HOWARD: Next time, I'll check the valve twice. Five times.

LACY: What if I asked you to?

HOWARD: You wouldn't do that.

LACY: I wouldn't. You know what I would and wouldn't do?

HOWARD: You're freaked out too. I recognize that, I was as well. But if you think about it...

LACY: Would you quit? If I asked you.

HOWARD: You married a stuntman. That's what I do. It's what I am. If I was waiting tables, would you have even gone out with me?

LACY: That's not the point. Now. Would you? ...If.

HOWARD: If you asked me.

LACY: Yeah.

(pause)

HOWARD: You won't ask me.

(pause)

LACY: You're serious, you're not quitting?

HOWARD: Honey, I'm not even considering it.

(HOWARD reaches up, arms wide, falls forwards...)

(As he does:)

BLACKOUT.

(Suddenly: LIGHTING FX: Flames flickering across the entire stage.)

(SOUND FX: Rushing, roaring noise.)

(YELLING VOICES - confused, distorted: CUT CAMERA! CUT CAMERA! SAFETY! WHERE'S THE SAFETY GUYS?... voices ad lib as they fade.)

END OF PLAY.

Tiger in a Cage

Cast: (1M, 1F)

HAROLD: M. Late twenties. Unable to sit still for very long. Edgy, twitchy… repressing.

PSYCHIATRIST: W. Young enough to still believe she can make a difference to the world - which makes it hard for her to remain unemotionally involved with her patients.

SETTING:
A jail cell.

TIME:
The play takes place in the present.

TIGER IN A CAGE received its premiere performance at the Rudyard Kipling Theatre Louisville, KY. March 2, 2007.

DARKNESS:

(A FEMALE VOICE grunts. High pitched, breathy, rhythmic grunts. Exertion.)

(A smacking noise - not immediately recognizable, but sexual. Deliciously sexual.)

(Grunt. Pause. Smack... ...over and over.)

(Louder.)

(The sounds cut off abruptly as:)

LIGHTS UP ON:

(HAROLD lying on the cot.)

(The SOUND of a steel doors rolling open, clanging shut.)

(The PSYCHIATRIST enters, carrying a case file, and a small folding chair.)

PSYCHIATRIST: Back again.

HAROLD: I didn't do nothing this time.

PSYCHIATRIST: And yet.

HAROLD: I guess they told you why.

PSYCHIATRIST: Actually, no. I was in the next building for a hearing, they dropped me a note, I came straight over. I wanted to hear from you first - I can read the police report later. But I wanted you to tell me.

(She shows him a document from the file.)

Whose signature is that?

HAROLD: Yours.

PSYCHIATRIST: Mine. On the bottom of a parole recommendation. I signed off on you, Harold.

HAROLD: I know. I didn't want to...

PSYCHIATRIST: To what?

HAROLD: I didn't do nothing.

PSYCHIATRIST: And yet. We were doing so well. You were doing so well.

HAROLD: I fell off the wagon.

(She gestures - continue.)

HAROLD: They put me next to the honeymoon suite.

PSYCHIATRIST: That sounds like a rationalization.

HAROLD: You don't understand, I been trying! ... I been trying. I was next to the honeymoon suite. That channel they have? I put a block on it. Downstairs, at the desk, even before I got to the room, I had'em block it. Guy looked at me like I was nuts. "It's a parental block," he says, "There's a code to override" I don't want the code, I tell him. ... I think he thought I was a nutcase - one of those religious types. And then this dickless wonder puts me next to the honeymoon suite. Half the night, banging away just the other side of the wall. I could hear everything. Voices, grunts – she was – I could hear her like she was in the bed, like right next to me. I couldn't take it.

PSYCHIATRIST: What did you do?

HAROLD: What d'you think I did? I went into the bathroom... and, you know... cut myself.

PSYCHIATRIST: We've discussed these kinds of –

HAROLD: I know! I know! I don't even keep a razor no more, I got a 'lectric one now and everything... but... I couldn't help it. I used those nail clippers. Two little parallel – they weren't even cuts, like little scratches. I screwed up again, didn't I?

PSYCHIATRIST: I'm not here to judge you, Harold.

HAROLD: Then what good are you? Tell me what I should've – What would you have done?

PSYCHIATRIST: That's hardly my –

HAROLD: If you don't tell me what's normal, how'm I gonna know? I want to get well.

PSYCHIATRIST: I want that too. We all do.

HAROLD: They don't. They want that chemical castration.

PSYCHIATRIST: It's a treatment therapy based on –

HAROLD: It's castration. That's what it is, that's what they want. They put the word chemical there so they can get away with it. They're sick. They're sick bastards.

PSYCHIATRIST: You need to sit down.

HAROLD: I know, I know. I'm good. ... You're the only one that ever believed in me. Believed I could get better.

PSYCHIATRIST: Did you believe that?

HAROLD: Yeah! Yeah, I know I.. I could. I just gotta know how. You gotta tell me. What would a normal guy have done?

PSYCHIATRIST: We've talked about channeling. Finding healthier outlets for your desires.

HAROLD: I didn't ask for it! I wasn't downloading pictures, I wasn't looking for it... I can't help hearing.

PSYCHIATRIST: You overheard a couple making love. And it aroused you. Did you consider masturbating?

HAROLD: You say that so clinical.

PSYCHIATRIST: I'm supposed to.

HAROLD: You're a woman, you should... You... you have beautiful breasts. I mean, I like your body.

PSYCHIATRIST: Now you're just avoiding. We talked about that. You're avoiding a situation you need to deal with.

HAROLD: I tried. I wanted to, really, I tried.

PSYCHIATRIST: But you were unable to.

HAROLD: It wouldn't work.

PSYCHIATRIST: Why do you think that was?

HAROLD: How the hell do I know! You're the goddamn shrink! They were banging, I was hearing it, and I wanted to but I couldn't!

(The PSYCHIATRIST backs up, alarmed.)

PSYCHIATRIST: Guard!

HAROLD: No, no, no... no, don't - you don't need... look, I'm sitting down. It's okay.

(Pause.)

(The PSYCHIATRIST looks through the barred door.)

HAROLD: He didn't hear you. He don't hear so good... It's okay. I'm over here.

(beat)

I tried that socializing.

PSYCHIATRIST: That's – that's good.

HAROLD: I went to a Starbucks, and I sat there for like two hours and I read a paper and I talked to people. Three people. No, four - this guy asked me what time it was. ... One woman smiled, and we talked. She talked to me.

PSYCHIATRIST: That's a big step.

HAROLD: But... I know it wouldn't work. I could never... you know... have gotten a hard-on. Not with her.

PSYCHIATRIST: Well not in a Starbucks.

HAROLD: I didn't mean –

PSYCHIATRIST: I know, I know... I was making a joke - but to illustrate a point. You are a long way from that stage. You don't need to worry about that.

HAROLD: I always worry about it.

PSYCHIATRIST: I know. What happened at the motel?

HAROLD: I don't want to talk about that.

PSYCHIATRIST: Then I can't help you. You want to get well, right?

HAROLD: I don't want them to castrate me.

PSYCHIATRIST: No one's going to do that.

HAROLD: I wanna tell you something.

PSYCHIATRIST: I'd like to hear it.

HAROLD: Really?

PSYCHIATRIST: Yes.

(Pause.)

HAROLD: I love you.

PSYCHIATRIST: Oh. Okay, well – now, that's not–

HAROLD: No, wait. I know you ain't supposed to be with a patient. I know that, I seen TV - but if it's like the patient's idea... I mean, I'm the one askin' you, right? I'm askin' you.

PSYCHIATRIST: Harold –

HAROLD: You can save me.

PSYCHIATRIST: I want to help you –

HAROLD: Listen. You said conversations. I talk to you. I talked to you every week I was here. I've talked to you more than anyone ever. I think I could - with you. It would work with you.

PSYCHIATRIST: Harold –

HAROLD: I'm not a bad guy.

PSYCHIATRIST: Yes. You are.

(Beat.)

HAROLD: But I don't have to be.

PSYCHIATRIST: No, I... You can change.

HAROLD: You can help me.

PSYCHIATRIST: I am helping you.

HAROLD: You can love me.

PSYCHIATRIST: No.

HAROLD: No?

PSYCHIATRIST: Never in a million years.

HAROLD: What did you say that for?

PSYCHIATRIST: You need to understand. This is a professional –

HAROLD: No, you need to understand. I love you. I want to... I want to kiss you. And hold you. And love you like a – That's new for me.

PSYCHIATRIST: Well... that's - it's a good thing.

HAROLD: Yeah?

PSYCHIATRIST: Not that way. Not in the way you want. But this is a big step for you, a very big step.

HAROLD: You could kiss me.

PSYCHIATRIST: I can't do that.

HAROLD: You don't think it would help me?

PSYCHIATRIST: Whether or not it might help you isn't the point.

HAROLD: Yes, it is!

PSYCHIATRIST: My job is–

HAROLD: To help me! And a kiss would help. Everything you've said about how I deal with – you know... okay, okay, okay... you know I could.

PSYCHIATRIST: What?

HAROLD: That guard... it takes him a while to get that door open, get down the hall, get this door open...

PSYCHIATRIST: Harold, I don't think –

HAROLD: I could kiss you right now. Whether you wanted me to or not.

PSYCHIATRIST: Okay, stop this –

HAROLD: You couldn't stop me. I could just grab you.

PSYCHIATRIST: Guard!

(She starts to rise... He lunges for her.)

GUA–

(She's cut off by his hand across her mouth.)

(He grabs her, wrestles her down on the cot.)

HAROLD: I could! I could, dammit! You gotta yell louder, that guard's deaf as post. He didn't hear you! He ain't comin'! He ain't comin', see? I could. I could right now, I could do anything and you can't stop me...

(She struggles violently, but to no avail.)

(He holds her down until she stops. A long moment.)

HAROLD: But I won't.

(He lets go of her, she flings him back, beating him away... but he's stepped back, out of reach.)

PSYCHIATRIST: GET THE HELL OFF ME!

HAROLD: I WON'T! I'm not gonna, 'cause... cause normal guys don't kiss no one that don't want to be kissed. You taught me that. You!

(He sits in the chair.)

You taught me that. So I ain't gonna do anything... but ask you. I'm changed, see? You did that. And you can save me. Just once. One kiss. I know in my heart that one kiss could save me. Like the frog in that fairy story - marries a princess. One kiss. I bet you kissed a hundred guys in your life. Two hundred. Guys in college, people you work with. Kiss'em hello, kiss'em goodbye. In France, they kiss both cheeks, just like shakin' hands. Don't mean nothin' to 'em. ... You can save me. You could make me... normal.

(She stands up, goes to the door... pauses.)

(Turns back ... and very gently, kisses his forehead.)

(Suddenly he grabs her, clutching her to him... but he's just clasping her, arms around her waist, holding his face close and sobbing into her belly.)

(She softens, touches his hair.)

PSYCHIATRIST: It's all right. You're going to be okay.

HAROLD: Nothing's okay.

(beat)

I lied to you. The noises. I thought it was the next room - but it wasn't. It was outside. In the parking lot.

(The FEMALE VOICE is heard again - quietly.

(Grunt. Pause, smack. Grunt, pause, smack...

(Harold gets up, walks to the window.

(The LIGHTING slowly CHANGES - dark in the jail cell, glaring bright through the window, shadows from the bars casting stripes across the scene.)

(The GRUNTING FEMALE VOICE gets gradually louder as he talks.)

HAROLD: I look out the window. I'm looking through the blinds, and the sun is bright. Stripes on my naked body. I'm like a tiger. I'm a tiger, waiting behind the window. Any moment, I could pounce. Any moment now. I can hear her. Then I can see her as I peer out from my lair. She's in a blue dress, her hair is pulled back, and she is glowing like the sun. She's... oh God... she's grunting. She's playing with a ball. She's throwing it as high as she can, up against the sky and catching it. Every time she throws her ball up in the air, she grunts... almost moans... huh! huh! huh! And her dress rides up on her leg, on her thigh. Each time she throws the ball up and when she reaches up to catch it, the edge of her dress pulls up. Higher. Glimpses of that tiny, perfect thigh. Huh! Huh! I'm a tiger. Oh yes... you little... you little perfect... meat.

(The noise stops.

(The lights revert to normal as he turns away from the window.)

HAROLD: I just watched her through the blinds. I never... I just watched. It was... incredible.

(Pause.)

PSYCHIATRIST: If all you'd done is watch, you wouldn't be back here.

HAROLD: I didn't touch her.

PSYCHIATRIST: I'm going to recommend a change of treatment. A course of hormone therapy. It's –

HAROLD: Chemicals. You're putting me on the chemicals.

PSYCHIATRIST: I have to get back.

(Beat)

Guard? GUARD!

(Pause.)

HAROLD: But... you kissed me.

(The guard enters to escort the psychiatrist out.)

PSYCHIATRIST: Yes. Yes I did.

(She leaves.)

(LIGHTS OUT on the SLAM OF THE DOOR.)

END OF PLAY.

Every Battle, Every War

Cast: (4 m)

LIEUTENANT: British, upper class accent. Very proper. *(note: the British pronunciation was leftenant, leading to "lefty" as a nickname for all officers of that rank.)*
TONKERS: London cockney. A coward.
NIGEL: Lower class English. Combative.
SKEETER: American, a southern redneck. Patriotic.

SETTING:
A muddy trench in a forward area.

TIME:
1916 - The War to End All Wars...
Later known as World War One.

EVERY BATTLE, EVERY WAR was first produced as part of AMERICAN HISTORY 101 by The Black Box Theatre Company in June, 2007.
The play was directed by Paul Messinger
Cast was as follows:
Nigel: Christopher Symonds
Lefty: Michael Symonds
Tonkers: John Frank
Skeeter: Morris Nash

IN DARKNESS:

(The sound of gunfire in the distance.)

(A HUGE EXPLOSION - close.)

(Flashes of light, a red glow.)

AT RISE:

(Three British soldiers huddle together in a trench - LIEUTENANT, NIGEL and TONKERS)

NIGEL: Bleedin' hell, Sir - that one was close!

LIEUTENANT: Steady there, chaps. The Bosch couldn't hit a double decker bus if they were riding inside it.

TONKERS: *(fearful)* Think we'll be goin' over the top soon, Lefty?

LIEUTENANT: In a hurry to be in the fray, are you, Tonkers? Good man. We'll be marching down the streets of Berlin by christmas time, you mark my words.

(A soldier in a US uniform runs on, scrambles next to them.)

SKEETER: Shoot, man! Where th'hell am I?

LIEUTENANT: Durham's light infantry - Fifth regiment.

SKEETER: Well sheee-oot, Ah'm loster than a turnip on a hog farm.

LIEUTENANT: I'm terribly sorry, I don't understand a word you're saying.

SKEETER: Don't 'pologize, man! I'm on yer side.

LIEUTENANT: Oh, you're American.

SKEETER: Hell yeah.

LIEUTENANT: Well, you're bloody late.

SKEETER: Late fer what?

LIEUTENANT: For the war, man! You should've been here two years ago.

SKEETER: I only jes' joined up last month.

LIEUTENANT: Well, try to be on time for the next one.

NIGEL: I 'eard this was the war to end all wars, sir.

LIEUTENANT: That's what they say. ...It would be nice to think so, son.

NIGEL: I mean - in't that what we're fightin' for, Lieutenant?

LIEUTENANT: We're fighting for King and Country, Nigel. The glory of the empire!

SKEETER: And mom's apple pie.

LIEUTENANT: What?

SKEETER: Fightin' fer mom's apple pie.

LIEUTENANT: I'm sorry, bit of the old shellburst tinnitus - I thought you said your mother's apple pie.

SKEETER: Sure did.

LIEUTENANT: That's what you're fighting for.

SKEETER: Yep.

LIEUTENANT: That's the most ridiculous thing I've ever heard.

TONKERS: I'll fight for some of me mum's rhubarb crumble, if it'll help.

LIEUTENANT: Shut up, Tonkers. You'll fight for King and Country.

TONKERS: Yes, sir.

NIGEL: *(to Tonkers)* Rhubarb crumble? Are you flamin' jokin', mate?

TONKERS: Woss wrong wiv me mum's crumble?

NIGEL: Ooh, aren't we posh - rhubarb bloody crumble. You should try me mam's sticky pudding.

TONKERS: Sticky pudding?

NIGEL: Better than yer mum's crumble.

LIEUTENANT: You're both fighting for King and Country, and there's an end to it.

NIGEL: Well, yes, sir. But if we was to fight fer - well, you know - I'd rather fight fer me mam's sticky pudding than 'is stuck-up rhubarb bloody crumble, no offense.

TONKERS: Just cause some of us 'as some standards –

NIGEL: You wanna shut it right now if you know what's good for ya!

LIEUTENANT: All right, chaps - stand down!

SKEETER: Maybe Ah'm slower than a pinchbug in molasses, but if I had my druthers, Ah'd fight fer yer boy's rhubarb thingy afore Ah'd fight fer yer dag-blamed King.

LIEUTENANT: Listen, if you want to be in our war, you'll fight for something serious. Honor is acceptable. Democracy - why not, you chaps seem to go in for that sort of thing. Taxation without representation, or whatever it was.

SKEETER: Truth, Justice and th'Merican way?

LIEUTENANT: Yes, well the American way seems to be to turn up two years late and shag our women while we do the fighting, so you might want to just focus on the truth and justice part –

SKEETER: And mom's apple pie.

LIEUTENANT: Will you stop talking about pie? You can't fight for pie. Nobody fights for pie.

SKEETER: Truth and Justice.

LIEUTENANT: Absolutely. But no pie.

SKEETER: Ah like pie.

LIEUTENANT: Yes, but you can't fight for it.

SKEETER: Ah'll fight you fer it!

LIEUTENANT: You will not! There will be absolutely no pie fighting.

TONKERS: What about mum's rhubarb crumble?

LIEUTENANT: Shut up about your mum's bloody rhubarb crumble!

(Nigel starts to speak)

Don't even think it.

(Nigel sags.)

SKEETER: Ah'm jes' sayin' - you can fight fer whatever. You fight fer yer pie or yer rhubarb - you fight fer Saturday night in a rumble seat with a cold beer. The "why" don't make no never-mind.

NIGEL: We're all against the hun, sir.

LIEUTENANT: It's not the same thing at all! Killing a human being - even a German one - is not to be enterprised lightly. To give one's life in the service of your country is noble. To get shot for pastry isn't.

(A whistle blows.)

NIGEL: The signal!

LIEUTENANT: It's time. Fix bayonets.

TONKERS: I guess this is it.

SKEETER: Well I ain't going.

LIEUTENANT: What?

SKEETER: I ain't going unless I can fight fer my mom's apple pie.

LIEUTENANT: They've given the signal.

SKEETER: Ah know why I'm here, and it ain't fer yer king.

LIEUTENANT: You'll follow orders, soldier.

SKEETER: Ah know where I stand, sir.

LIEUTENANT: Bloody Americans - always fighting for the wrong reasons.

SKEETER: Maybe - but we always win.

NIGEL: Sir - the signal.

TONKERS: They're fightin' the same enemy. Out in no man's land - how much do reasons matter? Like the man said - Every battle, every war...

LIEUTENANT: ... is fought for things worth dying for.

(beat)

(The Lieutenant blows his whistle.)

(Answering whistles sound - two, then ten, then twenty, off in the distance.)

LIEUTENANT: For King! For Country! FOR ENGLAND!

SKEETER: FER AMERICAN APPLE PIE!

TONKERS: FER ME MUM'S RHUBARB CRUMBLE.. AND TONKER'S MAM'S STICKY PUDDING!

NIGEL: AND CUSTARD! DON'T FORGET THE CUSTARD!

(They climb out of the trench and charge.)

(Machine gun fire.)

(As they fall -)

BLACKOUT.

END OF PLAY.

After It's All Over

Cast: (1F, 2M + recorded voice)

RECORDED BROADCAST - A radio news broadcast.

FATHER - Aware of politics and the outside world.

MOTHER - Aware of family relationship and the inside world.

SON - Late teenage. Naive but earnest.

SETTING:
A post-war survival bunker

TIME:
A hazy future.

AFTER IT'S ALL OVER premiered as part of the 2009 VIGNETTES OF THE APOCALYPSE at the Gene Frankel Theatre in New York City, February 12th, 2009.
The play was directed by Ilana Landecker.
Cast was as follows:
Father: Dylan Weinberger
Mother: Kristy Scheppke
Son: Amy Chang

DARKNESS:

RECORDED BROADCAST: *The war is over, the time for peace is at hand. In a recorded statement, the highest ranking surviving government official, the former intern of the deputy undersecretary to the National Endowment of the Arts and current Commander in Chief of the remaining Armed Force, Abigail Boniface, stated earlier today that the war is over. The United States, facing the overwhelming technology and insurmountable odds of the enemy forces, today declared unconditional surrender. This has been a recording. This message will repeat.*

AT RISE:

(MOTHER and FATHER wait impatiently.)

MOTHER: Maybe he stopped to look for supplies.

FATHER: Delays are to be expected. There's a war on.

MOTHER: The war is over. They keep saying it on the radio.

FATHER: I've heard a lot of things on the radio. Doesn't mean I believe them. We never surrendered in my day.

MOTHER: You think it's a trick?

FATHER: Let me ask you - this Abigail Boniface - do you think she's competent to lead an army to surrender?

MOTHER: Not much of an army. Before he got blown up, Reggie from the next bunker said we were down to six hundred National Guard reservists in Alaska. I could organize six hundred people.

FATHER: You'd have them all looking for cans of soup.

MOTHER: Better than charging up Bunker Hill with muskets when the enemy has laser sweeps and disinterays.

FATHER: We ran out of muskets years ago.

MOTHER: It was a simile.

FATHER: No it wasn't.

MOTHER: Or do I mean metaphor?

FATHER: God only knows what you mean, woman. I don't trust Abigail Boniface to surrender. She's probably pretending.

MOTHER: She's the government, she doesn't need to pretend.

FATHER: You can't trust the government. It's like what happened with the oceans.

MOTHER: That wasn't the government.

FATHER: But they lied about it! The enemy boils the entire ocean - cooks the sixth fleet and every man, woman and child within fifty miles of a shoreline - you could expect some coverage. What did they report? Minor damage in the Florida Keys. They boiled the ocean, woman!

MOTHER: Don't get all worked up.

FATHER: In Wyoming, it rained shrimp for three days.

MOTHER: Well, Wyoming...

FATHER: Cooked shrimp!

(beat)

You can't fight that. How do you fight shrimp? How do you launch a counter-attack when every navy vessel is too hot to touch?

MOTHER: I wish it would rain shrimp here. I could make gumbo.

FATHER: What is it with you and soup?

MOTHER: We've surrendered. A growing boy doesn't need a weapon anymore, he needs food.

FATHER: How do they know we surrendered?

MOTHER: Someone told them.

FATHER: Who?

MOTHER: Abigail must've sent someone.

FATHER: Who is there to send?

MOTHER: You're scaring me.

FATHER: I'm just saying.

MOTHER: Well, don't.

(Their SON enters, carrying a charred box of dented soup cans.)

MOTHER: Thank God you're back.

SON: I think God's dead. I saw part of his foot.

FATHER: We were – your mother was worrying about you, son.

SON: There's not much left up there. Some of the other bunkers... totally wiped. But I found soup.

MOTHER: You're a good boy.

SON: I found a whole case of it. Most of the labels are burnt off, but I think they're all chicken noodle.

MOTHER: There is a God. His name is Campbell's.

SON: I'm – I'm going out again.

FATHER: What?

SON: I ran into someone else. We kind of met up. We think, maybe we can launch a counter-offensive.

MOTHER: But the radio said... the war's over.

SON: We'll start a new one.

FATHER: With what?

SON: This kid knows how to build slingshots. With a slingshot, you can kill a deer with a rock.

MOTHER: Did you see any deer?

SON: No. But if we had, we could've killed one. We killed a rat.

FATHER: With a slingshot?

SON: No. The kid just dropped a rock on it. But the principal is the same. The slingshot adds a horizontal component to the rock's trajectory. You can kill more than a deer with it.

FATHER: Even the enemy?

SON: I don't see why not.

FATHER: They do have quantum battle-armor.

SON: Dad - that's for bullets and stuff.

FATHER: And napalm... and anthrax and sarin gas and atomic bombs –

MOTHER: They've got good armor, you gotta give them that.

SON: So they've got quantum battle armor! Big deal, there's probably a way to get through it. Every armor has a gap somewhere.

MOTHER: Big enough for a rock?

SON: It's worth a try.

FATHER: Your mom's just trying to look out for you, son. What worries me is... what will you do if you win?

SON: Defeat the enemy?

FATHER: Let's say, you and this slingshot kid –

SON: Rachel. Her name's Rachel.

MOTHER: Is she pretty?

SON: Mom –

MOTHER: I'm just asking –

SON: It's not like that.

FATHER: Let me finish.

MOTHER: I just thought maybe - you know. We could have grandkids. You could go fight a war next week.

FATHER: Let's say - for the sake of argument, you and Rachel find a chink in their quantum battle armor, and you find enough rocks to kill most of them.

SON: All of them, Dad. There's no shortage of rocks up there. You've forgotten what it's like on the surface. Without any trees or grass or plants anymore - all there is are rocks. Just lying around. We have a constant supply of ammunition.

FATHER: All right. You have the rocks, and you get past all the laser sweeps and those chaser mines, and the disinterays –

SON: And the slicers.

FATHER: What are –

SON: They're new. Silica nanotubes, hanging down from geostationary satellites. They're only a few molecules thick, so you can't see them. They swing around randomly - slice anything they brush into. Cut everything in a straight line for a hundred miles in a couple seconds. *Tseee-aow.* Go right through a person or a tank or a concrete bunker without slowing down.

FATHER: That's pretty neat technology.

SON: Can't get sharper than a slicer.

FATHER: Amazing.

MOTHER: Does she have a boyfriend?

SON: Mom! Please –

FATHER: So let's say you avoid the slicers - but you only kill most of the enemy.

SON: You mean, leave some alive?

FATHER: Even a few.

SON: If our arms got tired. Or the slingshot breaks... D'you think they'd surrender?

FATHER: They might.

SON: I'd hate to see that.

FATHER: But it's a possibility.

SON: I can't see the enemy surrendering. They never have before.

FATHER: They've never needed to.

MOTHER: It is their turn.

FATHER: Is it worth the risk?

(A pause.)

SON: We wouldn't accept it.

FATHER: Would Rachel?

SON: You should've seen that rat, Dad. She's a natural born killer.

MOTHER: She sounds like quite a catch.

SON: Mom - she's eight years old.

MOTHER: Oh. I thought she'd be your age.

SON: I'm like the oldest one left out there. She's got a pretty good eye for a kid, though. With her aim, and my strength - between us, we could do some damage.

MOTHER: So you both use the slingshot?

SON: We'll share it. I dunno, we haven't figured out how it all works. I can send the rock three times as far as she can, but she's much more likely to have it go towards a target.

FATHER: I just don't want them to surrender.

SON: Dad - we won't give them the chance to.

FATHER: Okay then.

SON: Okay.

FATHER: Son?

SON: Yeah?

FATHER: Try and find some more soup on the way back. Make your momma proud.

MOTHER: He doesn't need soup. He's going to win.

SON: I will.

(Their SON EXITS.)

MOTHER: Funny to think of the war ending.

FATHER: Yeah. Surrender... I can't see the enemy accepting a surrender. I know we wouldn't.

MOTHER: We don't need to.

FATHER: Maybe it's our turn.

MOTHER: Maybe.

(Lights slowly out, as the RECORDED BROADCAST rises.)

RECORDED BROADCAST: *... stated earlier today that the war is over. The United States, facing the overwhelming technology and insurmountable odds of the enemy forces, today declared unconditional surrender. This has been a recording. This message will repeat.*

END OF PLAY.

Better by Candlelight

Cast: (1M, 1 F)

MAN: 40's. Deceptively pleasant - with a sense of danger.

WOMAN: 30's. Almost perceptive enough to realize it.

SETTING:
A dark bedroom, lit by a single candle.

TIME:
The play takes place in the present.

BETTER BY CANDLELIGHT received its first production by the Rockland Theatre Company in Los Angeles, May, 2006.
The play was directed by David Shinebaum
Cast was as follows:
Man: David Shinebaum
Woman: Danielle Ozymandias

AT RISE:

Darkness

(A match flares - a candle is lit, barely revealing two figures and a bed.)

(The stage is largely dark - two figures moving in and out of a tiny pool of light, visible at the edge of the bed, but if they lie back they are shrouded in darkness.)

(A MAN and a WOMAN.)

WOMAN: Here. It's better by candlelight. You can believe anything.

MAN: How long have you had that candle there?

WOMAN: A while.

MAN: Sitting ready.

WOMAN: It's not like I planned –

MAN: You just happened to start putting a candle next to the bed.

WOMAN: There's a difference between planning and hoping.

MAN: I'm surprised there isn't a box of condoms next to it.

WOMAN: There's...

MAN: What?

WOMAN: There's actually some in the drawer.

MAN: You have condoms.

WOMAN: I'm allowed to have condoms.

MAN: Do you... do we need them?

WOMAN: What d'you mean?

MAN: Has there been anyone – no, forget it. I don't want to know. I don't even know why I'm here.

WOMAN: Look, we don't... this wasn't my –

MAN: I'm not in the mood.

WOMAN: You came over here.

MAN: I've changed my mind.

WOMAN: The box is unopened.

(Beat)

MAN: Unopened.

WOMAN: There hasn't been anyone since you.

MAN: Really?

WOMAN: Would I lie to you?

MAN: But you had them ready.

WOMAN: In case. I was hoping you would come back.

MAN: Why would you –

WOMAN: Have you?

MAN: I uh... I'm not –

WOMAN: I think you have. I think you should wear one.

MAN: You don't trust me.

WOMAN: Well it's not – I um... It's been a while.

MAN: A year. A year ago today.

WOMAN: Really.

MAN: Yeah.

WOMAN: So you should wear one.

MAN: You waited for me.

WOMAN: Yes, honey.

MAN: Sweetie.

WOMAN: Yes, sweetie. ... You need to wear one.

MAN: We never used to.

WOMAN: Well... It's been a while. Things have changed.

MAN: I don't want them to have changed.

WOMAN: Yeah, I noticed.

MAN: Do you still love me?

WOMAN: Is that what you want?

MAN: Tell me you do.

WOMAN: Are you sure?

MAN: I know that you – it doesn't matter. Tell me you love me.

WOMAN: I love you.

MAN: You still love me?

WOMAN: I still love you. I've always loved you.

MAN: I love you too.

(She opens the box. Paper tearing in the dark.)

WOMAN: I'll put it on for you.

MAN: I'm not... ready.

WOMAN: I can help with that.

MAN: I don't know if I can do this.

WOMAN: Relax. Hush... Jesus! Where did you get that scar?

(He sits up, hunching into the light.)

MAN: You know about that scar.

WOMAN: I'm sorry. I wasn't expecting...

MAN: You know about the frikkin' scar!

WOMAN: You're right... I... Honey, I forgot.

MAN: Sweetie.

WOMAN: Sorry. Sweetie. Look –

MAN: Forget it.

WOMAN: Listen, I was doing...

MAN: I know, I know.

WOMAN: I could do something else.

MAN: No. This isn't going to work.

WOMAN: Well I can't –

MAN: I know. I'm not asking for a refund. Keep the money.

(She removes her wig - looks at it.)

WOMAN: She must've been some lady.

MAN: Yeah, she was.

WOMAN: It's really been a year?

MAN: Yeah. Look, I don't want to talk about her.

WOMAN: Okay, but... you know, you paid for the whole night. Just 'cause it ain't quite what you wanted, hey... or we could just talk.

MAN: Talk.

WOMAN: Yeah. Talk. Some guys, that's all they wanna do anyway... So how did you get that scar?

MAN: I'm sorry, I–

WOMAN: Relax. I've seen worse, believe me. I had a guy once, he'd got shot there - seriously. Like in Desert Storm or something. Lost one of his nuts - guy was all messed up –

MAN: Really?

WOMAN: Yeah, you ain't got nothin' on that guy. I just wasn't expecting it, is all. I didn't mean to break character.

MAN: You were doing really well.

WOMAN: I used to do some acting. When I came to LA, I was gonna… well, whatever. So, 'fess up. Whatcha do?

MAN: Barbed wire fence. I was a kid. You know I forgot it happened?

WOMAN: You forgot that?

MAN: Yeah. Weird. I didn't remember it for years. My brain just edited it out. Fragments, maybe.

WOMAN: How old were you?

MAN: Eleven. Climbing over it. I was holding the wire down, stepping over and... it slipped. The wire twanged, rust flaked off, suddenly, the pressure was gone from my hand. I was gripping nothing but iron rust. Dust... grit in my fingertips.

WOMAN: That had to hurt like a sonofabitch.

MAN: Nah. I don't... I remember the sound - a low twang - like a loose guitar string. The slap. That sound, I remember that one too - the slap of barbed wire meeting denim... and the copper taste of fear... the sweat on my forehead that was dry moments before. I didn't really know what had – My body knew before I did. My body knew injury - not pain. No feelings - just sweat and a fear that tasted of pennies. The pain was later. Dull aches. Stomach clenching cramps... that was the next couple of days. All I knew then was sweat and fear and the dull twang of a barbed wire fence slipping from my hand like a rattlesnake.

WOMAN: Damn. You got it good!

MAN: Yeah.

WOMAN: I don't mean, you got it good - I mean, you know.

MAN: It got me good.

WOMAN: Right.

(Pause)

WOMAN: So, you wanna try again?

MAN: It's not... I can't. She's gone.

WOMAN: You're alright, man. You know that?

MAN: Thanks.

WOMAN: So, what happened with your wife? She leave you?

MAN: Kind of.

WOMAN: You're still carrying quite the torch for her.

MAN: Yeah. Can't let her go.

WOMAN: Hey... I've seen worse. I've always seen worse. That's the thing about me, I can be what you want. It's what I do. You don't have to pretend with me, because you can pretend with me.... and that's more real, in a way. You're allowed.

MAN: Tell you anything.

WOMAN: Anything at all.

MAN: You're a good woman.

WOMAN: Honey, I'm the best.

MAN: Sweetie.

WOMAN: Sweetie, I'm the best.

(She goes to kiss him... he hesitates.)

(She puts her wig on again. Kisses him.)

MAN: You always were.

(She pulls him back, onto the bed, onto her.)

WOMAN: So... what happened with her?

MAN: *(quietly)* Well... a year ago, we were in bed, and she... She called me by another guy's name. A guy I knew. I'd been... I was pretty sure anyway. But that just... I couldn't... so I... I don't know what came over... I took a knife. And I stabbed her. I couldn't stop myself – I just... I loved her so much. ... Hey, let me get that.

(He blows out the candle.)

END OF PLAY.

The Waiting Room of the Gods

Cast: (2M,2F)

CUPID: A grown man, out of shape, dressed in a diaper with a quiver of arrows on his back. Sick to death of both of his compatriots, Erato and Venus.

VENUS: Young, beautiful and seductive, dressed in a diaphanous gown. Sick to death of Cupid, but tolerant of Erato's foibles.

ERATO: A cheerful old lady, completely in her own world. Possibly while also in a wheelchair, using an old fashioned ear trumpet. No clue that she's tiresome to the others.

ED: In a word, spineless - including his physicality.

SETTING:
A very old fashioned waiting room.

TIME:
The play takes place in the present.

THE WAITING ROOM OF THE GODS premiered in Chicago at the Appetite Theatre's BRUSCHETTA 2009 SHORT PLAY FESTIVAL September 18th, 2009.
The play was directed by Dan Krall
Cast was as follows:
Cupid: Nathan Hicks
Venus: Megan Brown
Erato: Chris Genovese
Ed: Kevin Crispin

AT RISE:

(CUPID, VENUS and ERATO sit on dusty chairs in an antique waiting room. Bored.)

(ED enters.)

CUPID: Ah, crap. There's no room! Go away!

VENUS: Play nice.

(to Ed)

Hello.

ED: Hi.

CUPID: Sod off.

VENUS: Don't mind him - he just needs his diaper changed.

CUPID: Oh, you're so funny. How'd you like an arrow up your lute?

ERATO: Her what?!

CUPID: Lute. Lute!

(to Ed)

Deaf as a post.

ED: I'm not sure I'm in the right place.

CUPID: You a god?

VENUS: Of course he's a god.

ED: I'm not exac–

CUPID: Don't want any more muses.

ERATO: What did he say?

VENUS: He's calling you a muse again.

ERATO: Well if you think he is.

ED: I was told to wait here.

ERATO: Why?

ED: I'm not really sure how it all –

ERATO: He doesn't *seem* funny.

ED: What?

ERATO: Why is he so funny?

ED: Who, me?

CUPID: *(to Erato)* Shut up, you old bat!

ERATO: He's not at all amusing.

VENUS: No. Cupid was saying –

CUPID: You! You're a bloody muse, you shouldn't be here!

ERATO: *(to Ed)* How do you do. I'm Erato. *(brightly)* I'm a muse.

CUPID: He knows that, you harpy!

ED: Very pleased to meet –

CUPID: Quit lying to that withered up prune - are you a God?

ED: I'm –

VENUS: Stop being so elitist.

CUPID: It's a simple question.

ED: I'm not a god.

CUPID: I knew it.

VENUS: Are you a personification?

CUPID: Of course he's a bloody personification!

ERATO: Erato, the muse of Erotic Poetry... Of course, I don't get out much these days.

CUPID: Shut up!

VENUS: *(sympathetically)* You're not some awful sexual-politics satire are you?

CUPID: If he's the ghost of a gay marriage amendment with some moral to preach, I'm gonna stab him.

VENUS: You couldn't stab a pincushion.

CUPID: I will! I'll grab an arrow and just stick it in his – *(CUPID pulls an arrow from his quiver - but it is as limp as a piece of rope)* – what the hell is up with my arrow?!

VENUS: Apparently nothing.

CUPID: What is going on!

ED: Uh oh.

(Erato bursts out laughing.)

CUPID: That's not funny!

(Every time CUPID gestures, the arrow swings back and forth.)

ERATO: *(to Venus)* See if you can do something for that, dearie. *(to Ed)* She'll put a little starch in it. Venus. Goddess of sex.

VENUS: *(affronted)* And love. Sex and love. The mystical union –

CUPID: Bonking.

VENUS: *(yelling at Cupid)* THE SACRED CONJOINING OF TWO –

CUPID: KNOCKING BOOTS! She's the Goddess of all things sweaty and sticky.

VENUS: Oh, you make me so angry.

CUPID: God of love, here. *(he mimes shooting a bow)* Zip - boom! Above the waist - straight to the heart, every shot. That's love.

VENUS: You're a hallmark card.

(CUPID is speechless at this insult.)

ED: I'm sorry to butt in.

CUPID: *(to Venus)* You take that back.

ED: I think I might have caused some –

CUPID: You take that back right now! I was a god! A god, people worshipped me, they built temples!

VENUS: I had temples!

CUPID: Mine weren't filled with couches.

VENUS: Ooh!

ERATO: I could take a shot at it. I mean, I can't promise anything epic - but I could probably manage a limerick or two.

CUPID: What are you babbling about?

ERATO: Well, dear, it's all floppy.

CUPID: Poetry isn't going to help! ... This never happened before.

VENUS: Oh, honey, the times I've heard that one –

ED: I think... you know... maybe... perhaps my presence might've…

(A slow realization. EVERYONE looks at ED)

CUPID: What are you?

ED: I'm not a god... I'm...

CUPID: What. Are. –

ED: I'm Erectile Dysfunction.

(EVERYONE reacts)

I didn't ask to be here... there's all these new - Viagra, Cialis - it's... there's no room in the world for me anymore. They... they sent me here.

CUPID: You're a symptom! You should be down in a storage locker with chicken pox and a runny nose - this is a hall of Gods here!

ED: I didn't ask to be here.

CUPID: *(waving the arrow)* What about this?!

ED: That's what I do!

CUPID: Well that's just great.

ERATO: It's not as if you were using them, dear.

CUPID: Oh, thank you so much.

VENUS: It does seem strange - you being here.

ED: Well... guys think about me a lot. It's not just a medical thing, or a…

(beat)

First night failure. That's a biggie. You know how many teenaged whispered, fervent invocations are offered up to the heavens in that moment? The more they wish me away, the more they call out to me. Okay, it may not be the big time, it's not a sacred union... or love... or even a love poem. But it's a prayer. Where prayer is offered - belief forms. I never got marble temples, but you make do in the back seats of Buicks, and the beds of strangers after the bars have closed. Me and Bacchus, God of Wine? Like this. "You set'em up, and I'll knock'em down"... Not so much, these days. I mean, it's not that it doesn't happen anymore...

CUPID: People still fall in love.

VENUS: They certainly still do everything else.

ERATO: There once was a man from Nantucket –

CUPID & VENUS: Shut up, Erato!

ED: They just... they don't believe. They believe in pills.

CUPID: They lose their Gods. They move on.

VENUS: And we wait here.

(beat)

ED: So... I can stay?

CUPID: Do we have a choice?

VENUS: Pull up a chair, friend.

ED: Thanks. Call me Ed.

(THEY sit.)

ERATO: Are you staying long, dear?

ED: I guess so. I don't know.

VENUS: We come and go. It's the fashion of the times.

ED: I dunno. That viagra. They're not gonna give that one up easy.

ERATO: I could sing you a song. Cheer you up.

CUPID & VENUS: No songs!

ERATO: Passes the time.

(She sings)

The pears are ripe, and the leaves turn brown,

Hey derry, down derry, derry derry down,

The skirts go up and the trousers down,

Hey derry, derry derry down.

(The OTHERS gradually join in, eventually dancing around, twirling Cupid's floppy arrows in time.)

Three young maids went out in May,

Hey derry, down derry, derry derry down,

To meet the lads that make the hay,

Hey derry, derry derry down.

Farmer Dell had a lovely daughter,

Hey derry, down derry, derry derry down,

She never did just what she oughta,

Hey derry, derry derry down…

LIGHTS FADE AS THEY SING AND DANCE.

END OF PLAY.

The Fine Print

Cast: (1M, 1 Either)

ARCHIE: A somewhat mousy man. Precise, to the point of geekiness.

THE DEVIL: Elegantly dressed, and visibly the devil.

SETTING:
A kitchen in Archie's modest home.

TIME:
The play takes place in the present.

THE FINE PRINT received its premiere performance, and won the Audience Favorite Award at THE NEW PLAYS FESTIVAL AND COMPETITION, The Promenade Playhouse, Los Angeles, CA.
June 11th, 2009
The play was directed by Danielle Ozymandias
Cast was as follows:
The Devil: Michael Symonds
Archie: Christopher Symonds

AT RISE:

(ARCHIE reads a large document.)

(Behind him paces the DEVIL.)

DEVIL: It's a fairly standard contract.

ARCHIE: I always read them until I understand them.

DEVIL: Oh, for God's sake.

(Archie looks up, mildly surprised.)

DEVIL: I can say his name. I'm not frightened of him. ... Are you telling me you read every word of your cell phone agreement?

ARCHIE: Of course.

DEVIL: That's a first.

ARCHIE: Twice.

DEVIL: It's anal retentive, that's what it is.

ARCHIE: Saved me getting stuck paying for two more years if I took the quote unquote free replacement option in paragraph fourteen.

DEVIL: Yes, but if it takes you two years to read the contract, I fail to see any advantage.

ARCHIE: This is my immortal soul we're talking about here.

DEVIL: There's nothing in there about an immortal soul.

ARCHIE: Well, soul.

DEVIL: No one mentioned immortal, the contract says nothing about immortality - that would be stupid.

ARCHIE: Which is where I run into difficulty.

DEVIL: What don't you get?

ARCHIE: It all seems... mundane.

DEVIL: You think there should be fire and brimstone, and eternal damnation.

ARCHIE: This doesn't even mention an afterlife.

DEVIL: Jesus Christ! You're fixating.

ARCHIE: Could you not take his name in vain? I'm not dammed yet.

DEVIL: Take his name in vain? What does that even mean.

ARCHIE: Here we go again.

DEVIL: Listen. If you hit your thumb with a hammer, God really isn't bothered if you shout his son's name, even if you give him a new middle one beginning with an "F." Omniscient, remember? He knows the difference between that and an intentional beseeching prayer. That's not taking his name in vain.

ARCHIE: Then what is it?

DEVIL: It's nothing! It's like saying "Ow policeman!" The crime - and the ten commandments are a list of crimes - the crime is *taking* his name in vain. It's the same crime as impersonating a police officer. You dress up as a cop, and start ordering other citizens around - or fining them for speeding and pocketing the cash - that's a crime. Same thing. Pretending to be God - or to speak for God to make a quick buck - that's against his rules. Trust me, Jimmy Swaggart's gonna burn in hell. Metaphorically.

ARCHIE: Why do I feel you're being self serving?

DEVIL: Good God above, you're an irritating little man.

ARCHIE: Then why are you so keen on getting my soul?

DEVIL: You're fixating on this soul business. It's a word - I don't think there is a soul.

ARCHIE: And yet –

(Archie indicates the contract.)

DEVIL: Believe what you like - I've never seen one.

ARCHIE: You're the devil! Which leads me to two assumptions.

DEVIL: Why am I not surprised that you need to analyze it?

ARCHIE: Firstly, your existence proves there are supernatural powers. If the devil can appear before me, seeking to bind me to a contract, then God must also exist. Heaven, Hell - a struggle for my soul.

DEVIL: Man, what an ego.

ARCHIE: Secondly – secondly, you lie. You are the prince of lies, of deceit, of trickery. I cannot believe a word you say.

DEVIL: So why imagine that I'll hold to a contract?

ARCHIE: What?

DEVIL: If I'm the Prince of Lies, why do you think that I'll keep to a contract? 'Cause I signed it? I'm the devil, I'll sign my name to a dozen contracts, and then wipe my red behind with them. Ooh, I'm so evil.

ARCHIE: But you have to.

DEVIL: Only if I'm a man of my word. I'm not even a man.

ARCHIE: So why would I sign it?

DEVIL: Fame and fortune. That's what you wanted. People to know your name, the admiration of your peers.

ARCHIE: And love.

DEVIL: I explained –

ARCHIE: You're the devil.

DEVIL: I will talk to her. I can't guarantee she'll sign anything. Look, you'll be rich and famous. There'll be lots of opportunity - girls will be throwing themselves at you.

ARCHIE: I don't want girls.

DEVIL: You haven't even met them.

ARCHIE: I want Jenny back.

DEVIL: Yes, but as I explained –

ARCHIE: If you use your power –

DEVIL: It's free will! If you have it, she has it too. You have a choice - sign my contract, get riches, get ahead in life... Jenny will have her choice. She can be with a guy she no longer loves, but who is now very successful... Or not.

ARCHIE: She left me because I wasn't ambitious. She said I'd never amount to anything.

DEVIL: Then you can prove her wrong, and she'll come back. Right?

ARCHIE: She may have lied.

DEVIL: God, you have trust issues.

ARCHIE: This is my soul we're talking about here!

DEVIL: Metaphorically. Heaven and Hell are human creations. Fire and – have you ever even smelled brimstone? It's not that bad. It's like visiting the monkey house at the zoo, in five minutes, you don't even notice it – and yet – ooh, such a torture! You think that an ethereal soul can feel fire? Can smell brimstone? A soul has a nose?

ARCHIE: The torture is being deprived of God's love.

DEVIL: Well, that would be an issue to take up with him, then, wouldn't it? I don't care about the afterlife - if there is one. I only deal in the here and now.

ARCHIE: And I get fame and fortune?

DEVIL: At the cost of... let's say your reputation. A bunch of people you'll never meet - some who haven't even been born yet - thinking you were a bad guy. Why d'you care what they think?

ARCHIE: Like Hitler.

DEVIL: Not quite on that scale... Ego again.

ARCHIE: Eichmann?

DEVIL: Who?

ARCHIE: He was the architect that worked out the logistics for Hitler's "Final Solution." He figured out how to coordinate a genocide.

DEVIL: A man with a meticulous mind for planning. Detail oriented.

ARCHIE: I guess.

DEVIL: Probably read contracts twice.

ARCHIE: I'm not designing a death camp for you!

DEVIL: Who would ask you to? Besides, you're a systems engineer.

ARCHIE: Electrical systems engineer.

DEVIL: Exactly.

ARCHIE: *(thumbing the contract)* And you want me to design this circuit for you.

DEVIL: Exactly.

ARCHIE: It's so mundane.

DEVIL: It is.

ARCHIE: Most of its existing product.

DEVIL: Shouldn't even take you very long.

ARCHIE: There's facial recognition software running in every casino in Vegas. You walk in, two point four seconds later, they know who you are. They can pull up your driver license –

DEVIL: Credit history –

ARCHIE: Yeah.

DEVIL: So... doable.

ARCHIE: There are advantages to it.

DEVIL: That's where the riches part comes in. A systems upgrade. A huge contract from the military - you'll start with a promotion, soon be head of the department.

ARCHIE: I believe in what I do.

DEVIL: So do I.

ARCHIE: Remote weapons systems save lives.

DEVIL: I agree. There's no reason to put our boys in harms way if we don't have to.

ARCHIE: What's your angle?

DEVIL: I would like to reduce the psychological toll of warfare.

ARCHIE: We've been discussing that at the lab.

DEVIL: Think of this as a simple disconnect. Right now, there's some nineteen year old soldier, guiding his predator aircraft or driving his remote infantry track unit, steering with a joystick, blowing the hell out of the bad guys, and watching the events unfold through a TV monitor.

ARCHIE: Safely.

DEVIL: Only physically.

ARCHIE: I'm proud of my work.

DEVIL: When he - or she in such a modern army - presses the fire button, the screen shows what?

ARCHIE: Whatever they're shooting at.

DEVIL: Leading to psychological trauma. Moments of guilt, even.

ARCHIE: They're trained soldiers.

DEVIL: Oh, I know. Trained to kill. Do or die, my country right or wrong.

ARCHIE: Our products save soldier's lives.

DEVIL: At the cost of their souls.

ARCHIE: I thought you didn't believe in souls.

DEVIL: I think I said I didn't believe they had noses. I forget, I may have lied.... Facial recognition software. If the remote weapon can recognize targets and... eliminate them, without the operator ever having to see their faces... it would make the onus of a soldier less burdensome.

ARCHIE: You're the devil.

DEVIL: I thought we established that.

ARCHIE: So I design this circuit, and then something goes wrong, and our own boys get shot?

DEVIL: No. ... I mean - you need to design it right. But if a casino can tell exactly who you are by matching faces to a national registry of licensed drivers, don't you think you can design a weapons system that can tell the difference between an enemy combatant and a platoon of known individuals, all issued with whatever protective back up electronic signal you think up? It could be built into their dogtags. You could be the architect that ended the casualties of "friendly fire" forever. Just think... a U.S. soldier, operating a remote weapon from perfect safety, able to destroy whatever man, woman or child he's directed to - without seeing one drop of blood, without looking at one human face. And I'm not talking about indiscriminate carpet bombing with all the messy political implications, I mean one shot, one kill. One person - known, named, identified human being, completely removed of any humanity. Disposable. Killed without a single quiver of messy emotional consequence or human empathy. It's the final solution.

ARCHIE: But this is… we're already working on this!

(beat)

DEVIL: I know. Look at the last page.

ARCHIE: It's been – that's my name – hey, that's my signature! I never – I didn't...

DEVIL: You signed your soul away years ago.

(beat)

I have a confession. I'm not who you think I am. He's a little more discreet. I work for the other guy.

ARCHIE: Wait... You're an –

DEVIL: Don't say the "A' word. If you must, you could call me a guardian.

(beat)

He thought that maybe you – you of all people – should read the fine print.

(*Archie looks at the contract.)*

(LIGHTS SLOWLY OUT.)

END OF PLAY.

ABOUT THE PLAYWRIGHT

Arthur M. Jolly was born in the UK, and lived in England, Kenya, Madagascar and France until the age of eleven, when his family moved to New York City.

He was awarded the *Don and Gee Nicholl Fellowship in Screenwriting* by the Academy of Motion Picture Arts and Sciences in 2006, and lives and works as a screenwriter and playwright in Los Angeles.
His first play to be produced was *Howie's Last Words* - chosen from 850 submissions to be included in the prestigious *Summer Shorts Festival* by the Miami City Theatre in 2005. Future plays would be produced on both coasts, and from Miami as far north as Toronto. His full length play *Past Curfew* won the 2008 AOPW Fellowship, and his full length play *A Gulag Mouse* won the 2009 *Joining Sword and Pen* competition.

Upcoming productions and a complete bio and resume are available at ***www.arthurjolly.com***. He is represented by The Brant Rose Agency.

NOTES

5401151R00048

Printed in Great Britain
by Amazon.co.uk, Ltd.,
Marston Gate.